My C

Listen to Me Read
Book 4

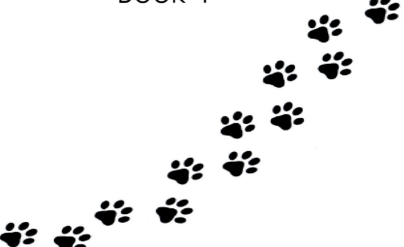

Written by **Annie Lena Day**

Illustrated by **Arabage**

Dedicated to my Grandson, Owen
and his cat, Cosmo ~

There is an old saying,
"When the cat's away, the mice will play."

But in this book,
"When the cat's **asleep,** the mice will play."

Copyright 2020 by Annie Lena Day Books

All rights reserved.

No part of this book may be reproduced in any form or by any electronic or mechanical means, including information storage and retrieval systems, without written permission from the author, except for the use of brief quotations in a book review.

ISBN 978-0-9600277-5-0

Dear Parents and Teachers,

This book is written for children who are beginning to read. Only a few sight words are needed and they are on page 5 (the Words Page).

Children also need to know the short a, e, and u sounds to "sound-out" a few words.

Please have your child read this book again and again. Repetition helps children learn and also builds confidence. So, encourage your child to reread this story to Aunts, Uncles, Grandparents, and as many enthusiastic family members as possible.

But most of all, ENJOY the book!

Annie Lena Day

Questions to Ask

Page 9   What do you think is behind the little door next to the bed?

Page 11   Who came out of that door?
Was your prediction correct?

Look for Patterns

1. When do the mice hide behind the mouse house door?
    (when the cat is jumping)

2. When do they come out to play?
    (when the cat takes a nap)

3. When the cat is jumping, notice the things in each room. Guess what the mice will play with while the cat naps?

4. What's funny about the last page?
    Is the cat sleep or awake?
    Why are the mice running?
    What do you think woke up the cat?

Words Page

my	jump	on
My	to	likes
in	a	like
	the	He

My cat likes to jump.

My cat likes to jump on my bed.

My cat likes to nap on my bed.

My cat likes to jump on a bag.

He naps on a bag.

My cat likes to jump on my hat.

He naps on my hat.

My cat likes the sun.

He naps in the sun.

Please visit the author's website
www.AnnieLenaDay.com
to find more books.

There are printables on the website too.

If you enjoyed this book, please leave a review so others can find it. Thanks!

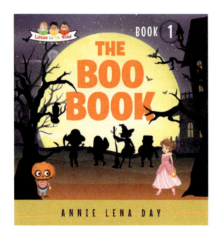 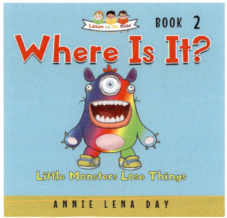 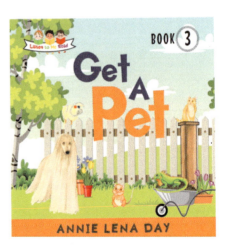

Made in the USA
Middletown, DE
11 October 2021